GEORGE HARGREAVES   MARY MARGARET JONES   GAVIN MCMILLAN

LANDSCAPES & GARDENS

ORO EDITIONS

Publishers of Architecture, Art, and Design
Gordon Goff: Publisher

www.oroeditions.com
info@oroeditions.com

Published by ORO Editions

Copyright © George Hargreaves 2015

All rights reserved. No part of this book may be reproduced, stored in a retrieval system, or transmitted in any form or by any means, including electronic, mechanical, photocopying of microfilming, recording, or otherwise (except that copying permitted by Sections 107 and 108 of the U.S. Copyright Law and except by reviewers for the public press) without written permission from the publisher.

You must not circulate this book in any other binding or cover and you must impose this same condition on any acquirer.

Graphic Design: Sally Roydhouse
Proofread by: Evan Morris
Production Supervision: Meghan Martin
Color Separations and Printing: Usana Shadday
Printed in China

10 9 8 7 6 5 4 3 2 1   First Edition

Library of Congress data available upon request. World Rights: Available
ISBN: 978-1-941806-70-8
International Distribution: www.oroeditions.com/distribution

For Glenn, our friend, colleague, and lover of gardens.
Chester Glenn Allen Jr. 1951-2011

George Hargreaves

Mary Margaret Jones

Gavin McMillan

Kirt Rieder

Catherine Miller

Ken Haines

Misty March

Brett Marsengill

Mary Lydecker

CONTENTS

Preface 9

Introduction 12

STRIATIONS
Discovery Green, Houston, Texas 17

WALL
555 Mission, San Francisco, California 33

ISLANDS
Stanford Science and Engineering Quad, Palo Alto, California 39
San Diego Waterfront Park, San Diego, California 47

RIBBONS
Haihe Waterfront, Tianjin, China 53
Piety Gardens, Crescent Park, New Orleans, Louisiana 69

NATIVES
Belo Garden, Dallas, Texas 77
Crissy Field, San Francisco, California 85

RAIN
Elizabeth Caruthers Park, Portland, Oregon 93

BACKGROUND FOREGROUND
Queen Elizabeth Park North, London, England 107
Queen Elizabeth Park South 2012 Gardens, London, England 124

Project Team Credits 140
Photography Credits 143

Preface
JULIA CZERNIAK

Gardens, parks, landscapes – these diverse scales and intensities of cultured nature all play important roles in our lives. This small collection is a provocative visual reminder of the enduring design potential of *landscape space as public space*.

Public gardens are tremendous assets. They act as treasured neighborhood gathering places, as cultural artifacts that reflect contemporary aesthetic concerns, and they foster appreciation for and knowledge of all things botanical: plant appearance, performance, behavior, care, and property—from the economic to the edible. Well-designed gardens reflect global concerns such as the role of biodiversity in the health of the planet and, more importantly, inspire public action on its behalf. Moreover, whereas parks are often mistakenly read as remnants of larger natural landscapes, gardens in their artifice conjure up loftier thoughts of publicness: of community, cultivation, self-sufficiency, and even democratic space where one sets aside differences in order to achieve common goals.

Hargreaves Associates remains committed to what they refer to as "unprogrammed space"—the innovative design of gardens, parks, and urban landscapes that are free from the extensive range of activities that support the city. As this collection argues and the projects demonstrate, landscape space is advanced as green space, characterized by form and process and articulated by a diverse range of trees, plants, and grasses, with paths to move on and places to sit. It is a valued and valuable program *in its own right* and, the designers argue, is what attracts people to the same public space again and again.

Not every garden, however, has such power to attract. Design matters. The design premises the following projects employ offer glimpses into many of the larger themes that have consistently produced the firm's successful work; a firm with an international reputation for its advanced design, technical expertise, public engagement, and the ability to get projects built in the context of complex politics and tough economics. These strategies, across scale, foreground connectivity, impassioned use, strong identity, and design innovation.

What follows is a more specific set of ideas—four organizational strategies (striations, walls, islands, and ribbons) and three themes (natives, rain, background/foreground)—that clearly articulates the design premises used to produce and exacerbate the immersive sensory experiences that are essential to enjoying, valuing, and measuring these types of landscape spaces. Circulation is one such measure. More than just movement corridors, these diverse organizations—generated through a nuanced reading of the site—create physical, visual, and site-specific relationships at nested scales between the body and the city and act as important supports for public life. Furthermore, these designs potently acknowledge the difference, by choices of edge conditions and plant robustness, between a public body and a private one.

The built work of Hargreaves Associates has the agency to accelerate positive change in the contexts in which they are located. It is optimistic that we—amidst the demands of the market and private development—consider these quiet green landscape spaces as part of this agency. It is even more noteworthy that we continue to value their design excellence as beautifully advanced here.

Julia Czerniak is a Professor of Architecture at Syracuse University, where she teaches architectural studios as well as seminars on landscape theory and criticism. Czerniak is educated both as an architect (M. Arch, Princeton University,) and landscape architect (B.A., Pennsylvania State University). Through her design practice, CLEAR, and her work at Syracuse University, her research and practice draw on the intersection of these disciplines. Czerniak lectures and teaches nationally and internationally. Her publications include *Large Parks* (Princeton Architectural Press, 2007), *Case: Downsview Park Toronto* (Prestel and Harvard Design School, 2001), and *Formerly Urban: Projecting Rust Belt Futures* (Princeton Architectural Press, 2013), and she regularly contributes essays to publications and magazines in the design field.

Introduction
GEORGE HARGREAVES

This little book is about landscapes and gardens in public spaces.

Public spaces are expressions of a culture's desire for common space, and most often the wish is for that space to be green. However, in today's world, public spaces are less and less likely to be created by public entities, and even in cases where they are, the maintenance required may suffer from funding cutbacks. In some cases private developers may be required to create public space as part of planning approvals. In others, a private group may form a nonprofit corporation for park development (or that private group may join a public entity to create a bonding capacity to raise funds for public space development). In any of these cases, the most frequently asked question is "How can the park pay for itself?" The truth is that parks cannot pay for all of their operating needs, but they can pay for some. On average we see around 25–35% as the highest amount of revenue a park can contribute to its own maintenance regime. This income is generated by park activities such as festivals, concerts and performances, corporate events, birthday parties and weddings, sporting activities, and food service—activities that require large areas of paving and other infrastructure that is often counter to the public's desire for green parks.

Based on the public input we have received in the many locales we have worked, we believe landscape is still the primary motive for public open space regardless of the varying programs and their intensities. So what does this say about the relationship between landscape and activities that produce revenue? Are they exclusive of one another? Is there a point at which the park or public space becomes more fairground than park? We believe the answers lie in the strength and robustness of the designed landscape. A successful park has loyal followers—people who identify a park with their culture, their region, their city, and their daily lives. This identification may be due to a particular activity in the park, but more often it is due to the gestalt of the overall park experience—said another way, the look and feel of the park. Landscape(s) can inspire through their visual qualities, tactile qualities, and contrasting or unifying qualities. They can inspire through their sustainability or their habitat creation, and they can inspire by providing human interaction with plants and wildlife. Through time it is the landscape that is remembered and privileged much more than income-producing programming. If we can produce landscapes for public spaces that embody these inspirational qualities, it will not matter when the programmed activities evolve, disappear (such as the 2012 Olympic games), or increase. History has shown us that, if it is done richly and robustly, a landscape can last for hundreds of years.

Embedded within the public's desire for green parks is a desire for gardens. Rich in semiology, gardens can be viewed as natural, agricultural, or cultural. Successfully placing any of these garden types in an urban context is quite different from the creation of private gardens for residences, estates, and other private settings. Public gardens cannot be fragile in their design or placement. Like the landscapes they inhabit, public gardens must be robust. They will not receive personalized maintenance, nor can they be subject to the overrunning pedestrian flows of large events or major gatherings. In addition to the selection of hardy plants and protection by slight grade separations or low barriers, the design of these gardens should be bold and somewhat simple, while retaining the very qualities that we enjoy so much—constant and changing colors, differing plant structures, and textures that change with the seasons or that carry the garden through winter. Gardens can inspire, provide refreshment, incite joy, or simply provide a provocative landscape context; as John Dixon Hunt wrote in regard to the landscape, "The garden is the highest aspiration of our culture."

The landscapes and gardens included here provide examples of different ways that this difficult balance of robustness and richness can be achieved in urban gardens set within public parks. Different design premises are employed that respond to the specifics of the context, be they structural, physical, or environmental, and form the book's chapters: Striations, Wall, Islands, Ribbons, Natives, Rain, and Background Foreground.

We hope you enjoy this little book.

STRIATIONS

The amount of active programs and buildings in Discovery Green in Houston, Texas, is quite intense for a 12-acre park. Although highly urban in its location and context, our goal was to build a strong landscape that over time would assert itself as the identity of the park. We were lucky to inherit a site-specific starting point: a mature allée of live oak trees. With the live oak allée oriented north to south, connecting downtown Houston to its convention center, we began to conceive the landscape as a series of striations through the site with program activities embedded in appropriately scaled intervening spaces. The landscape thus acts as a series of linear frames that can contain many things: major tree plantings, decks and walkways, gardens, water features, and lighting systems. Also, in some areas, we transformed the linear frame of landscape into an object-like garden through the use of plants that exhibit varying structures, colors, textures, and patterns. With over five years of maturation since the park's construction, the landscape has become the defining feature of an intensely active urban park.

Discovery Green
HOUSTON, TEXAS

Orange Key hibiscus.

Striations seen from above.

Existing live oak allée.

The gardens from above.

Dwarf maiden grass used as a contrasting element.

26

WALL

The South of Market area in San Francisco is comprised of oversized blocks. This plaza, or vest pocket park, at 555 Mission Street allows for pedestrian movement though the block and acts simultaneously as an outdoor room and open-ended sculpture gallery. The green wall is located along the entire mid-block to create a thriving vertical landscape where space and sunlight are at a premium. Plant selection is a mix of asparagus fern, black-eyed Susan vine, jasmine, violet trumpet vine, blood-red trumpet vine, and passion vine.

The planting creates an effect of high texture that contrasts with the refined materials of the plaza, which include granite and glass paving accented with polished wood furniture. In essence, the landscape is inverted—the wall as the lush green element and the ground essentially paved. The plants of the wall established quickly, and along with the addition of major artworks, led to this space having a completed look within a very short time after construction.

555 Mission
SAN FRANCISCO, CALIFORNIA

Violet trumpet vine, blood-red trumpet vine, jasmine, passion vine, asparagus plant, and black-eyed Susan vine comprise the plants of the wall.

WALL 35

ISLANDS

Most gardens are found in private or secluded settings; however, there is great interest by the public users of parks to enjoy the richness of plant materials that only gardens can provide. In this instance, two projects use the concept of gardens within islands, gardens set within high-traffic pedestrian spaces: a new quad at Stanford University and the San Diego Waterfront Park.

At Stanford, the new Science and Engineering Quad is primarily built over laboratories, which led to a highly paved space. The inspiration for the islands came from the original quad designed by Frederick Law Olmsted, which has a series of symmetrically spaced islands full of palms, trees, and shrubs. In this new quad we abandoned Olmsted's symmetry for a looser series of islands comprised of grass in some cases and richly patterned shrub and perennial plantings in others. Where possible, the islands accommodate heritage oak trees at native grade, creating sunken islands with terraced sides for shady retreats.

The San Diego Waterfront Park uses the island concept but with more free-flowing placement and forms. San Diego is geographically unique, with a climate that supports a broad array of plant materials. We sought to express this horticultural diversity in the gardens by using Mediterranean plants, tropical plants, and grasses to create a tapestry broadly sewn over the very informal islands. Less than a year old, the San Diego gardens are already thriving and will grow toward more vertical richness with time.

Stanford Science and Engineering Quad
PALO ALTO, CALIFORNIA

Firecracker penstemon, desert globemallow, and golden buckwheat create the structure, with highlights of redflower buckwheat.

Seaside fleabane.

Grass species of Berkeley sedge and nodding needlegrass provide a texture and color base for Frikart's aster and butterfly bush.

San Diego Waterfront Park
SAN DIEGO, CALIFORNIA

Grass gardens.

Mediterranean gardens.

RIBBONS

Haihe Waterfront Park, located west of Tianjin, China, and Piety Gardens, a part of Crescent Park on the New Orleans riverfront along the Mississippi River, are both long linear projects that reclaim abandoned industrial lands. Extended systems of landscape and pedestrian circulation are interspersed with moments of performance and program to create the backbone of each of these parks.

Haihe Waterfront Park is a "thickened edge" condition next to a dense central business district along the river. Comprised of layers, the park contains a double promenade, one for the city and one for the park, separated by a thick urban forest. The northern portion of the park is a series of landscape ovals, distinct from the ribbons of trees that flow through the park. The central portion consists of circulation paths that wind in and through the ribbons of trees, both of which continue through the park and connect to the geometric gardens and water voids that appear in the southern terminus of the park. Inspired by the vast nurseries along highways and rail corridors throughout the region, Haihe Waterfront Park has an agricultural and industrial look and feel from a distance. However, up close, the detail of the gardens is revealed, and, along with the layered tree systems, transforms this vast area into public parklands. Each ribbon and garden was thought of as distinct from one another, and therefore plant species of the same type are rarely found in the same location. Even though the very poor soil conditions were remedied, selected plant species had to be hardy and robust to survive the winds and other harsh climate conditions of this river corridor.

Piety Gardens had similar difficulties with soil conditions and high winds, as both the Tianjin and New Orleans sites are products of abandoned

Haihe Waterfront
TIANJIN, CHINA

industrial lands and big river environments. At Piety, we honed in on the railroad systems that formerly picked up and delivered freight transported via the river. Trees and circulation follow the historical rail curvature as the pedestrian paths progress to the wharf and along the extent of the park. Shrubs and perennials are grouped by color and plant type, with an arrhythmic dot pattern of plants mixed in-between groups—in homage to the home of the unique rhythms of American jazz.

Gardens featuring hollyhocks.

Gardens in the foreground of tree ribbons with yarrow, sedum, purple loosestrife, and mimosa trees.

Tree ribbons of Himalayan cedar, tree of heaven, Oriental plane tree, and Chinese tulip tree.

Chinese white poplar, pagoda tree, and desert ash trees.

Tree ribbons of Chinese willow, Oriental plane tree, and mimosa trees.

RIBBONS 65

Piety Gardens, Crescent Park
NEW ORLEANS, LOUISIANA

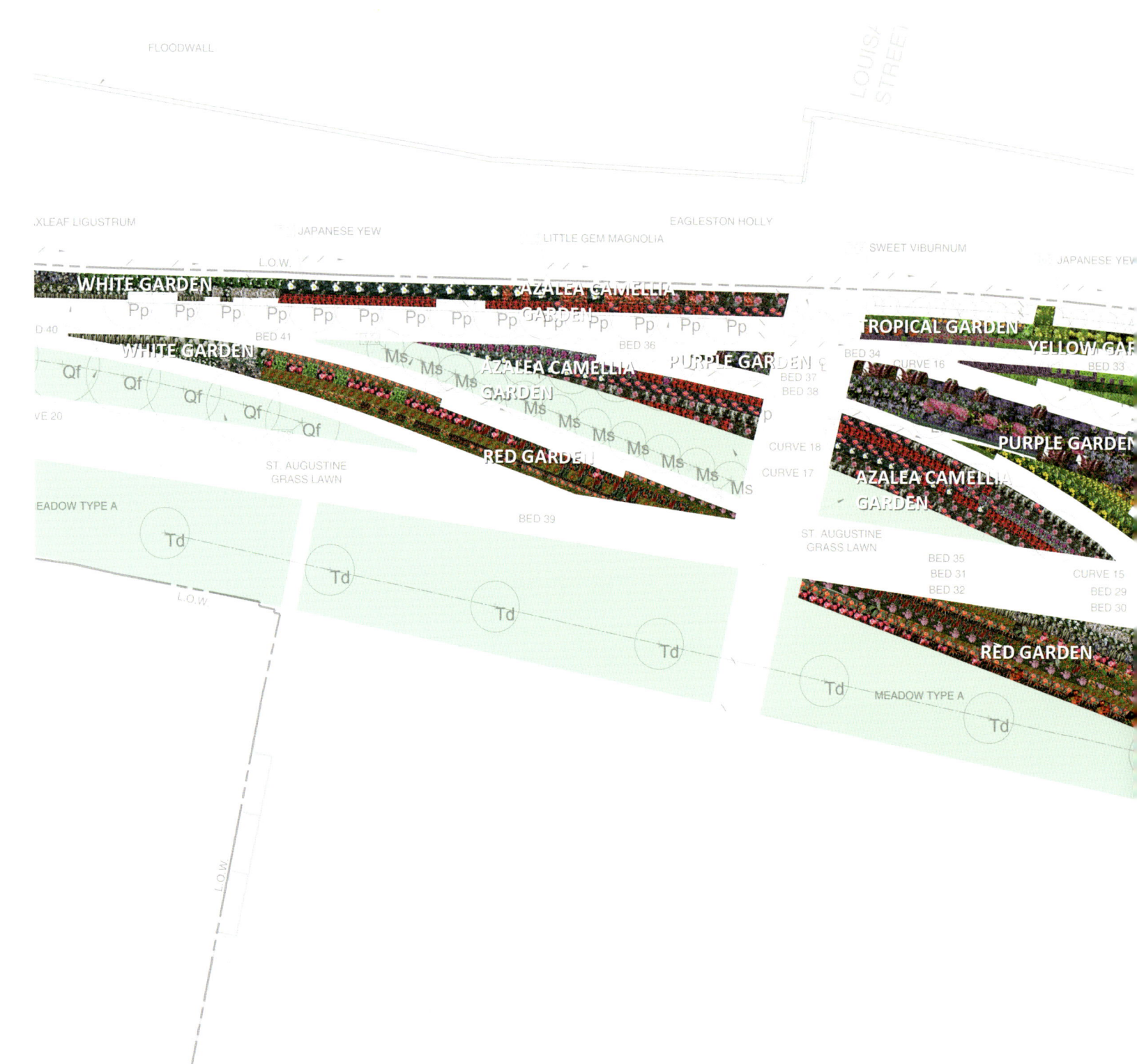

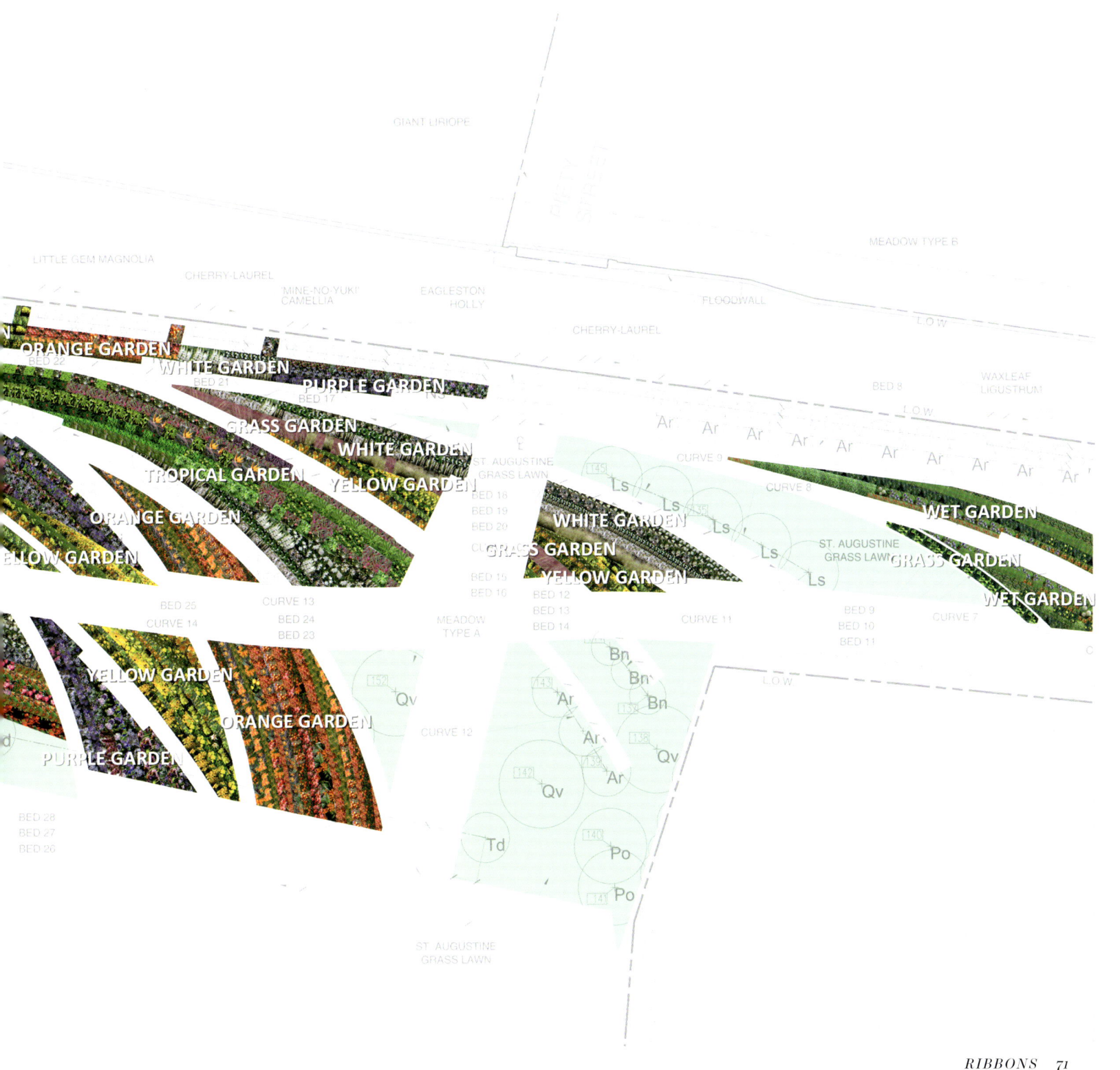

RIBBONS 73

NATIVES

The use of native plants is, to varying degrees, the Holy Grail for many designers and consumers. Here, two different projects, at different scales, take up that challenge. Belo Garden is less than two acres and lies in downtown Dallas, whereas Crissy Field is over 100 acres located at the foot of the Golden Gate Bridge in San Francisco's Presidio.

With the exception of the turf hill that provides a place for people to sit or gather, Belo Garden uses only native plants from the Dallas region. Grasses and perennials weave along and across circulation paths to give structure to the horizontal plane of the ground and create the effect of a tended prairie. Above, the trees signal passageway in and through the park, with a grove of clustered trees enhancing the secluded nature of the fountain, which is shaped in the pattern of leaves. The plants form a small, informal version of a botanical garden for some users, while for others the native plants inspire a certain genius loci to the park.

Crissy Field has several areas where native plants were exclusively used: around the introduced salt marsh, throughout the beach restoration, and in the back dune topography created along one edge of the park. The planting of the salt marsh was what we term a "landscape set in motion." The initial, fairly traditional planting, designed in response to the rhythm and movement of tides, has evolved in the 10-plus years since the project was constructed. The back dunes re-creation is highlighted with plants relocated by the National Park Service from back dune areas around the Bay. While not endangered, these plant materials are running out of natural areas in which to thrive. Again we see a landscape set in motion—if you look closely there is a good deal of evolution, but from a larger perspective it retains the intent and character of the initial installation.

One cannot help but notice that whether native or cultivated, many aspects of these gardens are indeed common: waving grasses exhibiting one set of textures and colors, with shrubs and perennials providing structure and a complementary set of textures and colors.

Belo Garden
DALLAS, TEXAS

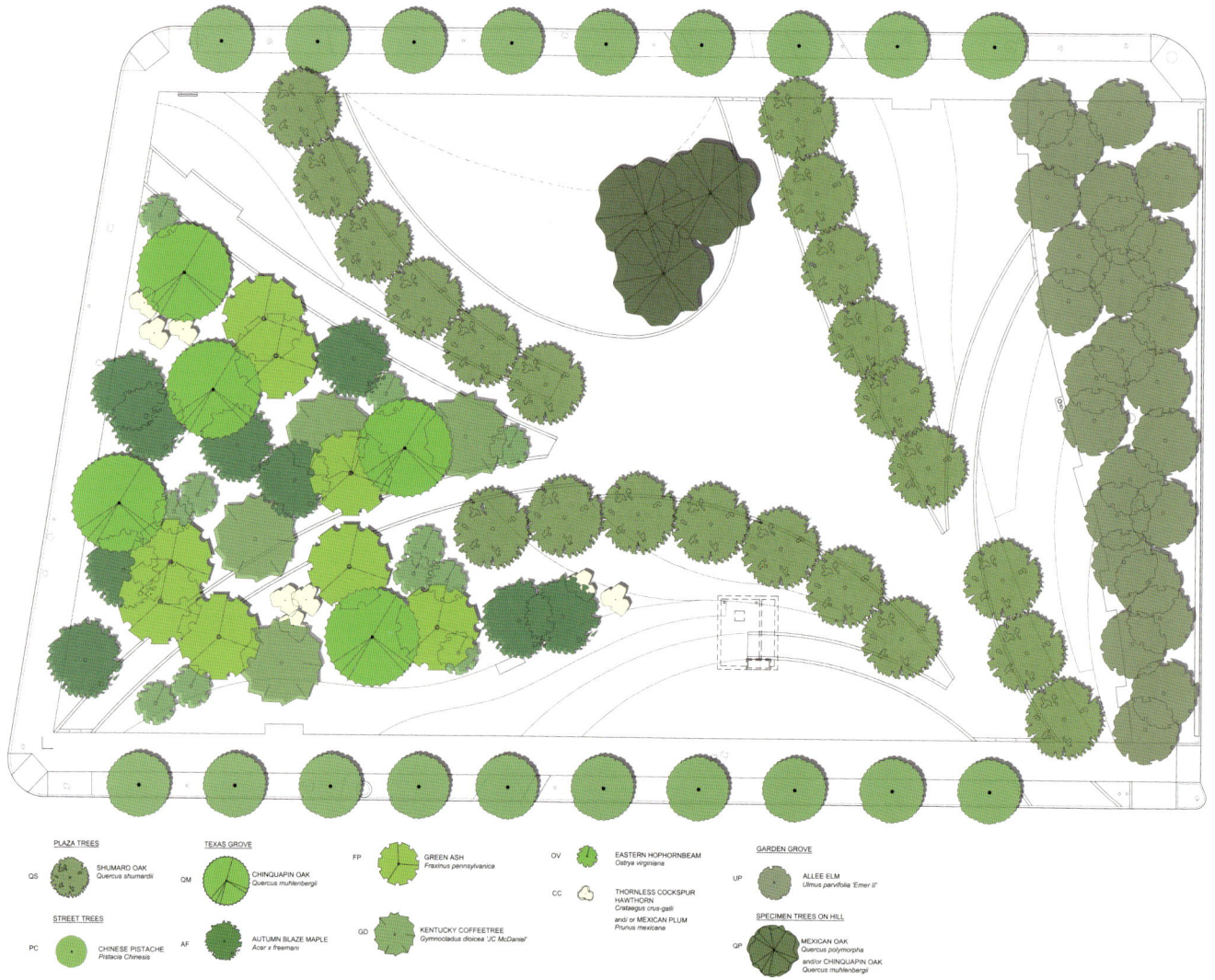

TREE PLANTING PLAN

GROUND PLANE PLANTING PLAN: SPRING

GROUND PLANE PLANTING PLAN: FALL

Goldsturm black-eyed Susan.

"Tended Prairie." *Weeping lovegrass, Adagio maiden grass, and little bluestem.*

Crissy Field
SAN FRANCISCO, CALIFORNIA

Chamisso bush lupine and coyote brush.

Field of back dune natives.

Marsh planting in motion. Willow, coyote brush, chairmaker's bulrush, rush, and saltgrass.

Chamisso bush lupine, common yarrow, and seaside woolly sunflower.

RAIN

Working in a planting zone that supports a great deal of variety is always fulfilling, but adding the dominate climate of the temperate rainforest of the Pacific Northwest leads to expressions in planting that are highly intrinsic. Elizabeth Caruthers Park in Portland, Oregon, is three acres and surrounded by mid-rise residential buildings with some retail on the ground floors. The center of the park is a village green that can host performances, festivals, markets, and public gatherings. To the north, play activities, picnicking, and similar activities are interspersed in sinuous bands of shrubs and perennials. The bands are sized to be large within their context and bold in texture and color. To the south, rainwater from the entire park is directed to four planted circular basins. Elevated boardwalks provide circulation through this wet landscape and allow continuous water flow while also providing protection for the wetland and water-loving plants. The wetland plants occur in and around the water basins, with water-loving plants radiating out in apparent randomness. While the sinuous bands in the north part of the park are bold and colorful with delicate textures, the wet planting areas take on the verdant green colors of the Pacific Northwest, expressed in big leaf textures.

Elizabeth Caruthers Park
PORTLAND, OREGON

Ivory Halo dogwood, Goldflame spirea, dwarf fountain grass, and allium.

Hidcote English lavender, Brilliancy rock rose, montbretia, and Goldflame spirea.

Dwarf fountain grass, montbretia, Brilliancy rock rose, and Ivory Halo dogwood.

Water basin with salal and common rush.

Sword fern, salal, common rush, and Pee Wee oakleaf hydrangea with the boardwalk arcing through.

BACKGROUND FOREGROUND

Queen Elizabeth Olympic Park is the most transformational project we have undertaken. The small, channelized, and polluted River Lea was transformed into the spine of the park. A large derelict section of London's East End formed the ground, which was made useable for the Olympic Games and parklands after two years of soil remediation. Our strategy, and that of our client, was to treat the Games as an overlay of venues and Olympic themes that would be removed after the Games with minimal retro-fitting for the legacy park. The landscape functions as both background and foreground depending on the perception of the observer—it is the background during events, but the foreground to those seeking nature or horticultural display.

As the river was cleaned, widened, and expanded with wetlands in the initial phase of construction, birds began to nest in and inhabit the wetlands, a clear demonstration of the habitat need. The river is accessed from the promenade at the upper bank level with gentle pedestrian pathways that flank a rain garden system—people and rainwater flowing to the river. The high volumes of soil that resulted from the construction on the site allowed us to create promontories and perched fields between the pathways, making places for people to gather. We cloaked the side flanks of these earthworks with highly diverse meadow plantings, with the plant species determined by the solar aspect of each slope. This created habitats in support of one of the goals of the landscape, to be as biodiverse as possible to enhance wildlife habitation. To that end, other habitats such as wet woodlands, valley-side woodlands, and birch stem woodlands were created in the north park. Eschewing the naturalistic, the various landscapes of the north park reveal their constructed qualities as well as their habitat value to the park user, proving the notion that people,

Queen Elizabeth Park North
LONDON, ENGLAND

wildlife, and habitat can be inclusive rather than exclusive. Rich in color at varying times of the year, including vibrant greens and fall colors, and full of dense and light textures, the park will be seen as a bridge between the 19th-century public park and a new type of park for the 21st century.

BACKGROUND FOREGROUND 111

Wet woodland.

North Park - Biozones

Key
- Trees and Scrub
- Wet Woodland
- Parks, Squares and Amenity Space
- Species-Rich Grassland
- Lawn
- Mixed Habitats
- Reed Bed
- Standing Open Water with Associated Swamp and Marsh
- Allotments
- Rivers and Streams

Labels: Wooded Gullies; Frog Ponds & Loggeries; Species-Rich Lawn; Bioswale Meadow; Birch Stem Woodland; Feature Meadow; Valley-Side Woodland; Wetland; Wet Woodland

Maiden grass, black-eyed Susan, aster, and sedum.

BACKGROUND FOREGROUND 117

Lupine, meadow buttercup, and dame's rocket.

The 2012 Olympic Gardens in the south park are a particularly British expression. We created an embankment of gardens along the River Lea in four sections. Each section makes reference to a time period of plant collection by British explorers and the hemisphere or continents they visited. While the planting varies between each segment, there was a common design language of bars, fitting to the linear site, of mixed shrubs, perennials, and grasses. Arcs of evergreen shrubs are interspersed within the bars, and all the elements are contained within fields of light, wispy perennials. The 2012 Gardens stand on their own as a celebration of a particular moment, along with past moments, in Britain's history, as expressed through plants and an evolving notion of the British garden.

Queen Elizabeth Park South
2012 Gardens
LONDON, ENGLAND

TEMPERATE ASIA, PARTICULARLY MONTANE CHINA, JAPAN, AND THE HIMALAYAS
19TH CENTURY, 20TH CENTURY

PLANTING TYPOLOGIES
KEY CATEGORIES:

- TREES & SHRUB SPECIES
- FORMAL CLIPPED HEDGING
- BOLD FOLIAGE STRIPS
- FLOWERING PERENNIALS
- DENSE VERTICAL PLANTING STRIPS
- TRANSPARENT / TALL EMERGENT PLANTING STRIPS

THE SOUTHERN HEMISPHERE, SOUTH AFRICA, AUSTRALIA, AND NEW ZEALAND
18TH CENTURY, EARLY 19TH CENTURY

- TREES & SHRUB SPECIES
- FORMAL CLIPPED HEDGING
- 'FIELD' PLANTING
- FLOWERING PERENNIALS
- DENSE VERTICAL PLANTING STRIPS
- TRANSPARENT / TALL EMERGENT PLANTING STRIPS
- BULB STRIPS

TEMPERATE AMERICAS
17TH CENTURY, 18TH CENTURY

- TREES & SHRUB SPECIES
- FORMAL CLIPPED HEDGING
- 'FIELD' PLANTING
- FLOWERING PERENNIALS
- DENSE VERTICAL PLANTING STRIPS
- TRANSPARENT / TALL EMERGENT PLANTING STRIPS
- BULB STRIPS

WESTERN EUROPE, THE MEDITERRANEAN, AND ASIA MINOR
15TH CENTURY AND BEYOND

- TREES & SHRUB SPECIES
- FORMAL CLIPPED HEDGING
- 'FIELD' PLANTING
- FLOWERING PERENNIALS
- DENSE VERTICAL PLANTING STRIPS
- TRANSPARENT / TALL EMERGENT PLANTING STRIPS
- BULB STRIPS

Bars and Fields in the Mediterranean gardens.

An arc of boxwood.

Southern Hemisphere garden with bars of agapanthus, African lovegrass, and torch lily.

BACKGROUND FOREGROUND 131

Northern Hemisphere with coneflower and prairie dropseed.

Southern Hemisphere.

Northern Hemisphere with button-snakeroot, coneflower, verbena, and switchgrass.

PROJECT TEAM CREDITS

DISCOVERY GREEN, HOUSTON, TEXAS
LEED Gold Certified
Client: Discovery Green Conservancy;
Guy Hagstette, FAIA, former President;
Barry Mandel, President and Park Director
Size: 12 acres (4.9 hectares)
Project Team:
Hargreaves Associates, Landscape Architects, Prime Consultant
Page Southerland Page, Architect and MEP
Lauren Griffith Associates, Associate Landscape Architects
Dan Euser Waterarchitecture, Water Feature Consultant
TSC Engineering, Civil Engineering
ETM Associates, Landscape Maintenance and Management Planner

Artworks:
Synchronicity of Color, by Margo Sawyer
Listening Vessels, by Douglas Hollis
Mist Tree, by Douglas Hollis
Monument au Fantôme, by Jean Dubuffet

555 MISSION, SAN FRANCISCO, CALIFORNIA
LEED Gold Certified
Client: Tishman Speyer
Size: 1 acre (0.4 hectares)
Project Team:
Hargreaves Associates, Landscape Architects
Kohn Pederson Fox Associates, Architects

Artworks:
Human Sculptures, by Jonathan Borofsky
Moonrise Sculptures: March, October and December, by Ugo Rondinone

STANFORD SCIENCE AND ENGINEERING QUAD, PALO ALTO, CALIFORNIA
Client: Stanford University; Jack Cleary, Associate Vice President, Academic Projects and Operations
Size: 8.5 acres (3.4 hectares)
Project Team:
Hargreaves Associates, Landscape Architects
BOORA Architects
BKF, Civil and Structural Engineering
ARUP, Civil and Structural Engineering

SAN DIEGO WATERFRONT PARK, SAN DIEGO
Client: County of San Diego, Department of General Services
Size: 12 acres (4.9 hectares)
Project Team:
Hargreaves Associates, Landscape Architects, Prime Consultant
Davis Davis Architects
Moffatt & Nichol Engineers, Civil and Coastal Engineering
Hope Engineering, Site Structural Engineering
Dan Euser Waterarchitecture, Water Feature Consultant

Schmidt Design Group, Landscape Construction Documents and Playground Design

HAIHE WATERFRONT, TIANJIN, CHINA
Client: Tianjin Binhai New Town Development Ltd.
Size: 74 acres (30 hectares)
Project Team:
Hargreaves Associates, Landscape Architects, Prime Consultant
Tianjin Urban Planning and Design Institute, Associate Landscape Architects
Skidmore, Owings & Merrill, Planning
Sherwood Design Engineers, Civil Engineers, Sustainable Design
Moffatt & Nichol Engineers, Coastline Infrastructure Engineering

PIETY GARDENS, CRESCENT PARK, NEW ORLEANS, LOUISIANA
Client: New Orleans Building Corporation, City of New Orleans;
Sean B. Cummings, former Executive Director
Size Phase 1: 20 acres (8.1 hectares)
Project Team:
Hargreaves Associates, Landscape Architects
Eskew+Dumez+Ripple, Executive Architect
Adjaye Associates, Architects, Piety Bridge
Michael Maltzan Architecture
Leibe Landscape Architecture, Associate Landscape Architect

Reinventing the Crescent Masterplan Team:
TEN Arquitectos
Hargreaves Associates
Chan Krieger Sieniewicz
Eskew+Dumez+Ripple

BELO GARDEN, DALLAS, TEXAS
Client: Dallas Park and Recreation Department, Willis C. Winters, Director; The Belo Foundation; Belo Corp.; Maureen H. and Robert W. Decherd
Size: 2 acres (0.8 hectares)
Project Team:
Hargreaves Associates, Landscape Architects, Prime Consultant
Carter & Burgess, Associate Landscape Architects
Dan Euser Waterarchitecture, Water Feature Consultant
ETM Associates, Public Space Management Planner
Texas AgriLife Research, Natural Resources Consulting

CRISSY FIELD, SAN FRANCISCO, CALIFORNIA
Client: Golden Gate National Parks Association; Greg Moore, Executive Director
Size: 100 acres (40 hectares)
Project Team:
Hargreaves Associates, Landscape Architects, Prime Consultant
Tanner Leddy Maytum Stacy Architects
Moffatt & Nichol Engineers, Civil and Coastal Engineering
E.G. Hirsch & Associates, Structural Engineering

PROJECT TEAM CREDITS

Rana Creek Habitat Restoration, Restoration Ecology
Philip Williams and Associates, Ltd., Wetland Hydrology Design
Wetland Research Associates, Habitat Biologist
National Park Service Natural Resources Staff

ELIZABETH CARUTHERS PARK, PORTLAND, OREGON

Client: City of Portland Parks & Recreation;
Zari Santner, former Director
Size: 2.1 acres (0.8 hectares)
Project Team:
Hargreaves Associates, Landscape Architects, Prime Consultant
Lango Hansen Landscape Architects,
Associate Landscape Architects
KPFF Consulting Engineers, Civil Engineering
Pacific Habitat Services

Artwork:
Song Cycles, by Douglas Hollis

QUEEN ELIZABETH PARK, LONDON, ENGLAND

Client: Olympic Delivery Authority;
John Hopkins, former Parklands and Public Realm
Project Director
Size: 274 acres
North Park: 110 acres (44.5 hectares)
South Park: 164 acres (66 hectares)

Project Team:
Hargreaves Associates, Design Lead, Master Planning
and Landscape Architecture
LDA Design, Prime Consultant, Master Planning
and Landscape Architecture
Dr. Peter Shepherd, Ecologist
Dr. Nigel Dunnett and Dr. James Hitchmough,
Meadow Horticulture
Sarah Price Landscapes, South Park Garden Plant Design
Atkins, North Park Engineering
Arup, South Park Engineering
National House Building Council, Sustainability Assessment
ETM Associates, Landscape Maintenance and
Management Planner

PHOTOGRAPHY CREDITS

George Hargreaves
Queen Elizabeth Park Cover, 113, 133
Crissy Field 84, 87

Robin Forster
Queen Elizabeth Park 2/3, 116,
122/123, 136/137
Courtesy of LDA Design.

Phil Askew
Queen Elizabeth Park 5, 125

Paul Hester
Discovery Green 6, 18, 20, 21, 22, 23,
24, 25, 26, 27, 28, 29, 30/31

Mary Margaret Jones
Queen Elizabeth Park 8

Hargreaves Associates and LDA Design
Queen Elizabeth Park 11, 114,
118/119

Andy Harris
Queen Elizabeth Park 14/15, 130

Jacob Petersen
Discovery Green 16

Kyle Jeffers
555 Mission 32, 34, 35, 36, 37;
Stanford Science and Engineering Quad
38, 41, 42, 43

George Waters
Stanford Science and Engineering Quad
40, 44, 45
Crissy Field 88

John Durant
San Diego Waterfront Park 46, 48/49,
50, 51

Zhuomin Peng
Haihe Waterfront 52, 54, 56, 57, 58,
59, 60/61, 62/63, 64, 65, 67

Stephen Houser
Piety Gardens, Crescent Park 68

Timothy Hursley
Piety Gardens, Crescent Park 72, 75

Jeremy Martin
Piety Gardens, Crescent Park 73, 74

David Woo
Belo Garden 80, 81, 82/83

Lara Rose
Crissy Field 89, 90

Bruce Forster
Elizabeth Caruthers Park 92, 94, 97,
98, 99, 100, 101, 102, 103, 104

Kurt Lango
Elizabeth Caruthers Park 96

LDA Design
Queen Elizabeth Park 106, 109, 110,
121, 131, 134, 135, 138, Back Cover

Olympic Delivery Authority
Queen Elizabeth Park 115

Bernward Engelke
Queen Elizabeth Park 126, 128
Courtesy of LDA Design.

Johanna Leibe
Piety Gardens, Crescent Park 144

All other images courtesy
of Hargreaves Associates.